Printed in the United States of America

Triumph

Through Life

30 Day Devotional

Aleisha H. Dubose

For those of us needing a little extra encouraging to push through.

Contents

From Me to You

Dear Readers:

Thank you for your interest in my work. This will be my first devotional, and I'm very excited to share it with you! My prayer for this devotional is that it encourages and inspires you each day you take the time to read it. I hope that by Day 30, you will be reignited and rejuvenated, having a new perspective on life and your relationship with Christ.

Yours Truly,

Aleisha H. Dubose

Introduction

Often times, we go through life not taking the time needed to gather ourselves in the midst of a tough day. It's easy to get caught up in negative thoughts, counterproductive conversations, and self-pity rather than turning to God for our troubles.

Day 1

God Knows

"I will provide for their needs before they ask, and I will help them while they are still asking for help."

Isaiah 65:24

Sometimes we feel like no one knows what we are going through and there's no possible way anyone could understand. God knows. He created us. He knows everything about us and feels our pain. Even when we feel we can't turn to family or friends; we should always remember we can go to God. We can trust Him to be there for us and provide comfort.

Last Thought:

God cares about our needs.

Day 2

Speak Life

You will live in joy and peace...

Isaiah 55:12

No matter what we're facing in life, we should speak life. *The tongue can bring death or life...Proverbs 18:21* There are mornings where I am very intentional in letting myself know that 'today is going to be a good day'. When we approach situations expecting the worst, sometimes the worst is what we get. We must recognize the power in our words and use them more wisely.

Last Thought:

Speak life to your situations.

Day 3

Just Call His Name

Now, may the Lord of peace Himself give you His peace at all times and in every situation...

2 Thessalonians 3:16

All we need to do is ask. He lets us know this in the book of John. *"You can ask for anything in my name, and I will do it, so that the Son can bring glory to the Father." - John 14:13* Now, granted, it is easy to forget this promise in the middle of a hard day. However, I feel it's completely worth ingraining in our memory. Whether I feel stressed with work or overwhelmed at home, if I go to Him and ask in His name, He will give me peace in my circumstances.

Last Thought:

He will give you peace.

Day 4

Protected

He will cover you with his feathers. He will shelter you with his wings. His faithful promises are your armor and protection.

Psalms 91:4

I had begun a sort of routine. Everyday after I left the school I would stop at either Cookout or McDonald's to kill the hunger while traveling to my next stop. On this day I had chosen to stop at Cookout. Big Mistake! There was only me and one other car in the drive-thru so at first, I thought I'd be able to get my food quickly and be on my way. Not a chance. I sat there for what seemed like a very long time. The first few minutes, I thought maybe the people in front had a big order, so I was fine with waiting a little. But then, the time seemed to get longer and longer! I was perplexed because this was a high traffic time, so by the time I would have left and went somewhere else, it would take even longer to get some food in my stomach. And I was extremely hungry! However, the frustration was starting to build. I could not bring myself to even begin to understand what was taking so long. What had they ordered?!

Finally, the other car got their food and it was my turn. The cashier apologized for the wait as she handed me my food. Now that I had my food, I was in a better mood.

So, I accepted her apology with a smile and went on my way.

As I turned out into the road, I saw flashing lights up ahead. All the way over in the right lane, there had been a wreck. It appeared that someone had been side swiped. The whole front side of where the car had been hit, was smashed. The thing is, that was the lane I would've been in because my next stop was the very next right.

God covered me under his wings by not allowing me to leave Cookout. He kept me out of harms way even though I could not see it at the time.

Last Thought:

When there are untimely delays in your schedule, have patience. It may be God ordering his divine protection to cover you.

Day 5

Oh Happy Day!

Rejoice in our confident hope. Be patient in trouble and keep on praying.

Romans 12:12

In the middle of hard times and struggle, it's easy to see the negative side of things and get fixated on them. We have to remember that God has our backs and our best interest at heart. *"For I know the plans I have for you," says the Lord. "They are plans for good and not for disaster, to give you a future and a hope." – Jeremiah .29:11*

Instead of heading into the day with dread, we can wake up saying, “Today’s going to be a great day.” In doing this, we have set our brain in motion to expect good things.

Last Thought:

Do your best to always maintain a positive outlook on life.

Day 6

Validated

The Lord will guide you continually, giving you water when you are dry and restoring your strength…

Isaiah 58:11

As a stepmom/bonus mom there are times when I question whether or not I matter in my daughter's life. I'll wonder to myself if she even cares about spending time with me or if I'm doing a good enough job holding up my end of the parenting. Am I being too hard on her? Am I punishing her too much? Do any of my words carry weight with her? Am I enough? In those moments when I start to feel this way and I'm about at my breaking point is usually when she'll come ask to stay the weekend with us or want to know if we can do something fun together. When this happens, I know that it's God comforting me and giving me the strength, I need to press forward. It's him letting me know: *"You got this, and I got you!"* And I am forever grateful each time he shows up for me in this way.

Last Thought:

Going forward today remember you got this, and God's got you!

Day 7

Undefeated

If God be for us, who can be against us?

Romans 8:31

About three years ago I was working as an associate at a large, well known store chain. During this particular time my husband had went back to school, and we were temporarily down one vehicle. For a while our schedules somewhat synced up, so we were able to manage. However, as you could imagine it soon presented certain challenges with us getting off at separate times and him needing to be in class by a specific time. So, one day I asked my area supervisor, after explaining our situation, if I could leave at 1pm (shift ended at 2pm) in order to have a ride home. She said yeah, so I told her bye and left. The next day when I came in, I was called to the assistant manager's office to discuss why I left early and without notifying anyone. You can imagine the confused look on my face as I calmly explained to our assistant manager what had actually happened. She only said that she wanted me to be aware of what had been said about me and thanked me for coming in to talk to her. Had our assistant manager believed the lies of my area supervisor, I could have been written up or fired. But God! He was with me. I know this because I didn't even get mad. I just walked out of the building laughing at the enemy for trying to come for me. He was not allowed to harm my position in any way, shape or form.

Last Thought:

With God on your side no one can come against you! They can try, but they WILL NOT succeed.

Day 8

No Limits

Let the beauty of the Lord our God be upon us and establish the work of our hands for us...

Psalm 90:17

Many times, we limit what God can do by only calling on him for the small things while trying to take on the bigger things ourselves. When we only seek God for things *we* feel he can fix, it is a reflection of just how weak our faith is in him. God can do anything! He can handle anything!

Ephesians 3:20 NLT says, *"Now all glory to God, who is able, through his mighty power at work within us, to accomplish infinitely more than we might ask or think."*

Last Thought:

Put all your trust in God and let him do what he does.

Day 9

Let it Go!

Be kind to one another, tenderhearted, forgiving one another, even as God in Christ forgave you.

Ephesians 4:32

Elsa had the right idea! We must let go of hurts, present and past, and learn to forgive each other.

I could not control my tears as I sat in bewilderment on my cousin's couch. We'd just found out that the nasty rumor about me that we had caught wind of was started by my own blood. Let's call him Ray. Ray and I had always been very close, so finding out it was him who started the rumor was like a knife to my heart. I did not understand why he would do such a thing.

I'm the type of person to build up walls once I'm hurt. All access is cut off to the one or ones who caused the pain, indefinitely. I did not speak to Ray for 3 years following that incident. I couldn't stand the sight of him, didn't want him to touch me, and it was very hard to be around him at all. Instead of talking to him, whenever he came around, I would start writing poems directed at my dislike for the person he was.

During the 3rd year of me alienating Ray, I began to notice just how much energy it was taking to avoid and dislike him. I felt like it was time to let it go and forgive. Although, I didn't like the thought of speaking and being around him still, I knew it was the right thing to do. It was also much healthier than holding on to a 3-year-old grudge. So, I forgave him, for me.

Last Thought:

Only when we forgive, can the healing start to take place.

Day 10

Hakuna Matata

Don't worry about anything; instead, pray about everything. Tell God what you need and thank him for all he has done.

Philippians 4:6

In the movie *The Lion King* Timon and Pumbaa encouraged Simba not to worry about things he couldn't control. While their methods may have been a little misguided, there was some truth to what they were saying. Worrying is no good for any of us.

According to WebMD, worrying excessively can lead to high anxiety and cause physical illness. God is aware of all the many stressors in our lives. Instead of focusing in on these things, he instructs us to pray. When we turn to Him instead of allowing worry to overtake us, we give Him permission to comfort us.

Last Thought:

Don’t let your worries be bigger than your prayers.

Day 11

Believe

By His wounds you are healed.

I Peter 2:24

In my youth, I suffered from headaches constantly. Sometimes, the pain would be so severe, it would bring me to tears (I would later find out this was because I needed glasses). One day when I was about 8 or 9, I felt a headache trying to come on. I remember going in our bathroom, looking in the mirror, placing my hand on my head and asking God to heal me and remove the pain. Instantly, the pain left! To be completely honest, it startled me. Being a P.K. (preacher's kid), I was taught to pray and lay hands on myself, but I guess at that age I simply could not comprehend how it all worked. Nevertheless, I was healed, and it helped to build my confidence in prayer and faith.

Last Thought:

Rest in this truth today. You are already healed, because He took those stripes for us.

Day 12

Chosen

God the Father knew you and chose you long ago, and his Spirit has made you holy... May God give you more and more grace and peace.

1 Peter 1:2

Wherever you are in life at this moment, know that God chose you for this specific time and place. You were handpicked by Him to complete this task. It's no accident that you succeed with ease.

You were made for this! Don't be discouraged by mishaps and missteps that may surround you but move forward in power and prayer with purpose.

Last Thought:

There is power in living and moving within your purpose.

Day 13

Trust Your Prayers

Whatever things you ask when you pray, believe that you receive them, and you will have them.

Mark 11:24

Like every other week, we paid all of our bills before setting aside any money for extras. Usually we'd have it measured out where there'd be enough left over to buy groceries for the week. This particular week we laser focused in on paying off some of the big bills that were coming due. Thankfully, we were able to pay them off. Unfortunately, that left us with no extra money for food or gas. The fridge was empty, and the gas tank was on E. So, I did what I knew to do. I got by myself and prayed, "Lord, you know our situation, we need your help." A little while later I felt the urge to check our bank account. There was $360 that showed up out of nowhere. We were able to go to the store, stock up on groceries, and fill up the tank. Once we arrived back home, my husband decided to tempt fate by ordering something offline. Payment was rejected! As quickly as we had restocked and refilled, the money was gone. The account had returned to $0.00. God provided us with just enough to take care of our necessities.

Last Thought:

Our prayers will go further with some faith behind them.

Day 14

When He Says Yes

And we know that all things work together for good to them that love God.

Romans 8:28

February 14, 2012. That was the day my hubby and decided to tie the knot. My dress was on the way, hair appointments made, and guests invited. Everything was set. The only thing that stood in our way was our department supervisor D.P. who did not want to give both of us the same day off. After it was explained to him why we wanted this day, his response was, "I can let one of you off but not the other." You can imagine the look of confusion on my face. How in the world could we get married with only one person being let off! But there was a ram in the bush. One of the guys who worked in the same area as my husband offered up his day so we could both be off. I don't know who it was, but I am forever grateful for his kindness.

Last Thought:

His *yes* goes beyond any *no* you may encounter.

Day 15

Careful, Not Careless

So, let's not get tired of doing what is good. At just the right time we will reap a harvest of blessing if we don't give up.

Galatians 6:9

Making the daily choice to do the right thing can be a hard one. Especially, with all the craziness we encounter in dealing with our spouses, kids, bosses, co-workers, etc. It's easy to get caught up in a heated moment of disagreement and say things we never meant to say, allowing emotions to take over.

There will always be circumstances in our lives that may throw off our mood for the moment or even our entire day, but it's how we respond that matters. Someone might cut you off in traffic, or maybe the cashier at the store was ridiculously rude without cause. Maybe your boss gave someone else the promotion that you felt you deserved. Or you've just gotten home from work and want to relax, but your husband/kids have left clothes all over everything. These are just a few possible triggers that take place in our lives that may cause us to forget who we are and whose we are.

The most important thing to remember in these instances is that the way we respond can alter the outcome of the situation.

Last Thought:

Deny your emotions the right to rule anything in your life and respond with the love.

Day 16

Expiration Date

"I am leaving you with a gift—peace of mind and heart. And the peace I give is a gift the world cannot give. So, don't be troubled or afraid."

John 14:27

With God on our side, we don't have to allow the troubles of the world to trouble our spirits. While certain situations may present themselves as a cause for concern, we should not be frazzled by them. Philippians 4:7 says, *"Then you will experience God's peace, which exceeds anything we can understand." (NLT)*

The troubles and unfortunate events we experience and endure in life, all have an expiration date. They're not meant to last forever. If we remain focused on this truth, we can inhabit peace.

Last Thought:

His peace will outlast your troubles.

Day 17

Lean In

So, let us come boldly to the throne of our gracious God. There we will receive His mercy, and we will find grace to help us when we need it the most.

Hebrews 4:16

Absolutely nothing is too hard for God! Think about a situation that almost took you out. Remember how exhausting it was? All the tears shed. How you were on the verge of throwing in the towel and had almost lost all hope? But you made it through! You were able to overcome that thing that had you in such a devastating funk because of His grace.

So, in the days to come, rejoice in knowing that His grace will be there for you. It's there for our benefit. All we have to do is go to Him.

Last Thought:

When the going gets tough, lean into his grace.

Day 18

Speak Up

"Now go; I will help you speak and will teach you what to say."

Exodus 4:12

What can I say? How will I say it? Will it be received in the right way? These are just a few of the questions that go through my mind whenever I feel the need to talk with someone. Whether it's an encouraging word, a sympathetic word, or even a mentoring word, I want to say the right things that won't lead others astray.

While this particular scripture is God talking to Moses, I believe these are His words to us as well. He will give us the words we need and help us to construct and deliver them in a meaningful way that would fulfill whatever it is we're trying to accomplish.

Last Thought:

Trust His guidance and speak up!

Day 19

Thanks a Lot!

Be thankful in all circumstances, for this is God's will for you who belong to Christ Jesus.

I Thessalonians 5:18

One thing our parents instilled in us growing up was to always be thankful for what we had. Whenever my brother or I complained about not liking certain dishes that was set before us, we'd immediately hear about those less fortunate who wish they had anything to eat.

Then, there were times when (like all children) we'd get upset with our parents and want to seclude ourselves from them. At which time, we'd be swiftly reminded how blessed we were to have parents who cared about us.

Whenever we appeared to be ungrateful about anything, our parents made sure we understood why this behavior was inappropriate. They not only taught us to be thankful, but *why* we should be thankful as well.

I believe those talks are what laid the groundwork for the gratitude I now carry for life and everything in it.

We can all be grateful for life, family, friends, enemies, etc. We can be grateful because God is good, and He gives us favor that we don't deserve. We should be thankful because of his mercy towards us and his everlasting love.

Last Thought:

Try to pinpoint three things today that you are grateful for beyond family, friends, spouse, or kids.

Day 20

Heart Tales

Take delight in the Lord, and he will give you the desires of your heart.

Psalm 37:4

Have you ever sat down and made a list of all the things you truly desire? I've done this often over the years. Being a writer, it's one of the things I enjoy.

Towards the end of my high school career, I created a list that included qualities I felt were a must have for my ideal husband. Not many people new about this list, but I held it dear to my heart. Everyone I dated from high school and beyond got measured against this list. I knew what I wanted, even though I didn't have a plan for how to achieve it. But God knew my heart and blessed me in-spite of my poor choices, and inconsistencies to do what was right. It's great to know that we can't earn His blessings. He blesses us because He wants to and it's just who He is.

Looking back, I must say that He truly gave me the desires of my heart. I now have a husband who can cook, has a sense of humor, is a man of God, a great father, respects me, is caring but also if anything were to go down, capable of providing the protection we need.

He did that, and I am forever grateful! I'm a living witness that He will give you the desires of your heart according to His will.

Last Thought:

Write down your heart's desires, pray over them, and watch God move.

Day 21

Level Up

For you know that when your faith is tested, your endurance has a chance to grow.

James 1:3

As I pulled into the gas station, with just enough funds for gas and groceries, I noticed a guy searching for an open pump. Before I began putting gas in my car, he pulled in, and as I looked up, he was looking at me as if he had a question. He asked if I could spare him a couple of dollars to get gas because he was on E. In my mind all I could think was '*I only have enough for me.*'

However, my second thought came from a scripture verse that I had heard many times: *"when you did it to one of the least of these my brothers and sisters, you were doing it to me!" -Matt 25:40* I knew what I had to do. So, I gave what I could, and he was very appreciative.

Even though initially, I struggled with the decision to help, in the end I'm glad I was able to assist someone in need. Looking back, that incident was a test of faith. Would I almost deplete my funds to help someone else? Would I deny the needs of my family, trusting God to see us through? I almost didn't, but I'm glad I did. God took care of our household and we did not go without. I was still able to get enough food to feed my family.

Last Thought:

Don't be stressed when your faith is tested.

It simply means it's time to level up.

Day 22

Light Work

Nothing is too hard for the Lord.

Genesis 18:14

No matter what the situation looks like or feels like, God can handle it. Sometimes we try to compare God to ourselves and put Him on our level. We think if it's too hard for me then I shouldn't trouble God with it, but that's literally why He's there. He comes to give us grace and take on those burdens that we're unable to bear. He takes the brunt of the hits, in order to minimize our pain.

If we could put all miracles in perspective, both past and present, we must conclude that God is greater than any obstacle we could imagine. Our God is bigger, greater, and stronger than any person, place, or thing that would threaten to dismantle us.

Last Thought:

What may seem big to us is light work to Him.

Day 23

Stronger Together

So be strong and courageous, all you who put your hope in the Lord!

Psalms 31:24

Growing up in the '90's, I used to watch Mighty Morphin Power Rangers. It was a show about six teenagers who dressed in weaponized suits to take on bad guys.

The interesting thing was that they would often get beaten when they fought separately, causing their courage to wane. It wasn't until they joined forces as one unit that they became strong enough to defeat their opponent and have their courage restored.

When we put our hope and faith in God, we are joining forces with Him. He gives us strength and courage to take on any situation. In Him we are mighty!

Last Thought:

Don't try to attack life alone. He's there waiting to be tagged in, to be your strength.

Day 24

Smile

Stop being angry! Turn from your rage! Do not lose your temper—it only leads to harm.

Psalms 37:8

Being angry does not benefit us or God in any way. James 1:20 tells us exactly how He feels on the matter *"Human anger does not produce the righteousness God desires."* Anger is unproductive and can be exhausting when handled improperly. In James 1:19, it reads, *"...be quick to listen, slow to speak, and slow to get angry."* God wants us to be equipped with skill and knowledge of how to handle such a strong emotion.

If you're like me (and I pray you're not) sometimes you might wake up angry, not even understanding why, what happened, or who did it. During these times it's important to search out the cause and get to the root of why you're feeling this way.

For me, anger, when it happens usually stems from either a dream I'd had the night before or an unsettled disagreement between my husband and me.

Perhaps you find yourself in similar scenarios. I encourage you to think of three things that make you smile and meditate on them.

Last Thought:

Create a list of things that bring a smile to your face, so you always have them to go back and look at during tough days.

Day 25

Cheer Up!

A cheerful heart is good medicine, but a broken spirit saps a person's strength.

Proverbs 17:22

I have always been told that laughter is good for the soul. Upon recent studies, I have found that it's apparently good for the entire body. According to helpguide.org laughter can relieve tension, stress, and boost your immune system.

It's no wonder why God instructs us in His word to be cheerful. He knew the benefits it would bring to our health. He designed it that way.

Most times when things come in and disrupt our lives, it's hard to control feeling sad or upset. But we have to remember that we can control them.

Yes, there are good days and not so good days, but even in those tough days we can will ourselves to be happy or cheerful.

Last Thought:

Life is short. Choose to be grateful.

Day 26

Power Trip

For God has not given us a spirit of fear and timidity, but of power, love and self-discipline.

2 Timothy 1:7

Fear is not from God. When it shows up in our lives, we must rebuke it and cast it out.

We have no reason to fear any trial, tribulation, temptation, circumstance, or situation that would attempt to reap havoc in our lives.

God has given us power. By definition, this, means we have the ability to influence the course of events happening around us.

Although, He has entrusted this power to us, it is up to us to decide if we will walk in it or walk in fear.

Last Thought:

Resist fear by operating in power.

Day 27

Winner's Circle

With God's help we will do well...

Psalms 60:12

There are days when we feel like giving up, but we must overcome that feeling. The enemy would love nothing more than for you to give in to the overwhelm in your life. Don't give him that satisfaction.

Hebrews 13: 5 says, *"...I will never fail you. I will never abandon you."*

Stand firm in the truth that God has our back, front, and side. He has us covered. Knowing this, we can dismiss any feelings of defeat that may try and consume us.

We must accept our positions as winners because He has already defeated the enemy. Walking in victory has to become not just a saying, but an attitude that we wake up with daily.

Last Thought:

You will succeed with His help!

Day 28

Better Days Ahead

Those who plant in tears will harvest with shouts of joy.

Psalms 126:5

In those times when circumstances in life brings us to the point of tears, it can feel like it's never-ending. Burdens get heavier. The dark times seem longer and even darker. But these times won't last always.

Weeping may last through the night,
but joy comes with the morning.

Psalms 30:5

Knowing that the pain and sorrow won't last provides an optimistic hope for the future. It gives us something to look forward to providing us with a sense of comfort.

Last Thought:

When you're feeling down and out and can't see a way through, know that better days are on the other side of your troubles.

Day 29

Attitude of New

"I have told you all this so that you may have peace in me. Here on earth you will have many trials and sorrows. But take heart, because I have overcome the world."

John 16:33

We can overcome anything because he already has. He wants us to have peace.

During the beginning of my teen years, I would get picked on for certain clothes and shoes I wore to school. One day in 7th grade, I can recall this group of girls standing in front of the lockers watching everyone pass by. The moment I passed by them I heard, “Uh oh, she finally got some new shoes y’all.” I didn’t show it then, but I was mortified. It made me super aware that I stood out and everyone could see me. In those days, I gave a lot of thought to what others thought of me. It really bothered me on an unhealthy level.

Then one day, an upper classman in my Wednesday night Bible Study class, spoke a word to me that forever freed me from these thoughts. She told me it didn’t matter what you did, good or bad, somebody would always have something to say. This was a revelation to me. I hadn’t even considered it. My only focus for so long had been how to keep people from talking about me. Her words literally changed my life.

Of course, I'm human, so there have been moments where I would find myself caring what others thought of me. But the words of that young lady in my Bible Study class always pulled me right back. I believe God used her to help me overcome and ultimately be delivered from the thoughts of people.

Last Thought:

Change your perspective, change your life.

Day 30

Fearless

"Don't be afraid, for I am with you. Don't be discouraged, for I am your God. I will strengthen you and help you. I will hold you up with my victorious right hand."

Isaiah 41:10

It's easy to allow fear to take over when we're unsure of what might happen now or in the near future. Whether in the next few minutes or the next few years, not knowing what's about to happen can cause major anxiety. We can't waist time wondering and worrying about what's next and if we'll be prepared for what may come. Instead, we need only to trust God to guide our feet and show us the way. We have His word that he is with us always.

Last Thought:

Stay encouraged because He is with you.

Words to Live By

Above all else guard your heart, for it is the wellspring of life. -Proverbs 4:23

Respect and obey the Lord! This is the beginning of wisdom. – Proverbs 9:10

Stupidity is reckless, senseless, and foolish. – Proverbs 9:13

You will be safe, if you always do right, but you will get caught if you are dishonest. - Proverbs 10:9

Hatred stirs up trouble; love overlooks the wrongs that others do. -Proverbs 10:12

Many are helped by useful instruction, but fools are killed by their own stupidity. - Proverbs 10:21

The Lord hates anyone who cheats, but he likes everyone who is honest. -Proverbs 11:1

A gossip tells everything, but a true friend will keep a secret. -Proverbs 11:13

A beautiful woman who acts foolish is like a gold ring on the snout of a pig. – Proverbs 11:22

People with understanding control their anger; a hot temper shows great foolishness. -Proverbs 14:29

Sensible people control their temper; they earn respect by overlooking wrongs. -Proverbs 19:11

Don't make friends with quick-tempered people or spend time with those who have bad tempers. Proverbs 22:24

If a wise man has an argument with a fool, the fool only rages and laughs, and there is no quiet. -Proverbs 29:9

Affirmations

I am in charge of my emotions.

I will go confidently in the direction of my dreams and live the life I have imagined.

God fills my life with overflowing good!

-unknown

I can conquer any obstacle in my path.

My life has meaning.

"I can face things that are out of my control and not act out of control." -Lysa Terkurst

God is my strong fortress, and he makes my way perfect. 2 Samuel 22:33

As He guides me, my strength is renewed.
Psalms 23:3

God's power works best in my weakness.

2 Corinthians 12:9

Though I am surrounded by troubles, you will protect me. Psalms 138:7

The Lord will work out His plan for my life.
Psalms 138:8

He shows me loving-kindness and forgives my sin. Hebrews 8:12

I am happy for what I have because of Him.

I Timothy

He gives me rest when I'm tired.

Matthew 11:28

Acknowledgements

Thanks to my hubby for reminding me to take a break and enjoy life.

Thanks to my parents for encouraging me to push through my writer's block.

Thanks to award winning child author Felicia Lee. Your advice helped to redirect my focus.

Check out her books:

Audrey Lost her Shoe & I Can Be

Made in the USA
Columbia, SC
26 May 2025

58384653R00052